Protesters wave the West German flag at the Berlin Wall
while East German border guards look on.

Cornerstones of Freedom

The Story of
THE UNIFICATION OF GERMANY

By Jim Hargrove

The flags of East and West Germany hang on the Berlin Wall.

CHILDRENS PRESS ®
CHICAGO

Fireworks rise over Berlin's Brandenburg Gate in October 1990
as Germans celebrate unification.

Library of Congress Cataloging-in-Publication Data

Hargrove, Jim.

   The story of the unification of Germany / by Jim
Hargrove.
      p.   cm. — (Cornerstones of freedom)
   Summary: Discusses the historical background and
events leading up to the reunification of a divided Germany
and the political and economic ramifications.
   ISBN 0-516-04761-2
   1. Germany—History—Unification, 1990—Juvenile
literature. [1. Germany—History—Unification, 1990.]
I. Title. II. Series.
DD262.H37 1991
943.087'9—dc20   91-12650
                                                     CIP
                                                      AC

PHOTO CREDITS
AP/Wide World Photos—4, 6, 8 (left), 14, 15 (2 photos), 16
(2 photos), 17, 21 (2 photos), 23, 25, 27 (right), 29 (2 photos),
31
Black Star—© 1979 Stern, 13
© Virginia R. Grimes—3, 19 (left), 26, 32
H. Armstrong Roberts—2, 5 (right)
Journalism Services—© Fotex/I. Röhrbein, 1; © Fotex/
Lothar Kruse, 18 (right)
National Archives—5 (left)
Photri—8 (right), 10 (left); © Mauritius, 18 (left), 19 (right)
Reuters/Bettmann Newsphotos—20, 27 (left)
UPI/Bettmann—7, 9, 10 (right), 13 inset
Valan—© A. Diem, Cover
Cover - Brandenburg Gate, Berlin

At midnight on October 3, 1990, church bells rang throughout Germany. Millions of people stayed up through the night to celebrate a historic event. After forty-five years of division, the German nation was officially made whole again. A formal flag-raising ceremony in Berlin marked the end of a political separation that dated back to the end of World War II.

In 1945, the forces of Germany's Adolf Hitler were defeated by the armies of the Allied nations. Among many other countries, the Allies included the United States, the USSR, Great Britain, and France.

When World War II ended in Europe, the German nation was divided into four occupied territories. The four territories were controlled by American, Soviet, British, and French military governors. The

Adolf Hitler (left) led Germany into a disastrous war. A sign in four languages (right) proclaims the division of the defeated nation's capital.

5

city of Berlin, which lay deep in the Soviet zone, was also divided by the four powers. Allied leaders agreed to reunite the four regions a few years after the end of the war.

Almost immediately, however, the Soviet governors began squabbling with the other Allied governors. Eventually, the Soviet leaders broke the agreements they had made. They decided to keep control of a number of Eastern European nations, including the zone they occupied in Germany.

Within a matter of months, Russian troops began building a fortified border. The border divided the nations of Eastern Europe, controlled by Russia, from the independent nations of Western Europe. This heavily guarded border—866 miles long—cut Germany into two sections—east and west.

On March 5, 1946, the British statesman Winston Churchill said, "An Iron Curtain has descended across the continent." The Iron Curtain was the longest armed fortification in the world. To the west of it were independent nations, most with democratic forms of government. To the east were nations suddenly dominated by the Soviet Union. Under Soviet-style communism, none of the Eastern European nations would be permitted to hold meaningful elections for decades.

On May 23, 1949, the German zones occupied by American, British, and French forces were merged. They became an independent nation: the Federal Republic of Germany (FRG), usually known as West Germany.

The World War II Allied leaders (left to right) Winston Churchill, Harry S Truman, and Joseph Stalin agreed to the postwar division of Germany.

ES LEBE
DIE NATIONALE FRONT
DES DEMOKRATISCHEN
DEUTSCHLAND

The new government of East Germany was formed in 1949. Barbed wire (inset) separated the two Germanys.

On October 7, 1949, the Russian zone of Germany officially became a new nation named the German Democratic Republic (GDR). However, the creation of an official East German state was a mere formality. Long before 1949, the Iron Curtain had isolated East Germany from West Germany.

Over the years, the Iron Curtain was reinforced so that it was almost impossible to cross it without the permission of a Communist government. The barriers across Europe eventually included steel, cement, and barbed-wire fences lined with deadly mine fields and explosive booby traps. Watchtowers along the walls housed electronic spy equipment and troops armed with machine guns and other weapons, all readily at hand.

8

In 1961, a second "Iron Curtain" was built, this one entirely inside the borders of East Germany. The Berlin Wall, as the new fortification was called, divided the huge city of Berlin in half. East Berlin was run by the Communist government of East Germany; West Berlin was run by West Germany.

The Iron Curtain and the Berlin Wall were built to keep people inside. Many people in Eastern Europe, including East Germany, wanted to live in the democratic nations of Western Europe, which included West Germany. In the West, where the free enterprise system thrived, people could run their own businesses, hire people to work for them, and, if successful, earn a good living.

East German construction workers laying sections of concrete for the Berlin Wall.

Under the Communist governments of Eastern Europe, including East Germany, the free enterprise system was virtually outlawed. Central governments controlled every aspect of economic life, and few people had the right to form private companies. Before many years passed, it was clear that most people in democratic nations could earn a better living than most people in Communist nations.

Unfortunately, the Iron Curtain worked. The people of Eastern European countries were prevented from moving to the West.

Those who tried to cross the Iron Curtain without permission faced possible death sentences if caught. Nevertheless, thousands of people risked their lives trying to flee to the West.

Floral wreaths at the Berlin Wall recall those who died trying to escape. Right: The body of a young man killed while crossing the wall is carried back to the East.

In the late 1970s, for example, two East German friends began planning their escape. One was Gunther Wetzel, a construction worker who lived with his wife Petra in the town of Possneck. The other was Peter Strelzyk, an electrician who lived nearby with his wife. Both men had children. Both men dreamed of freedom and a better life in West Germany.

A television program about hot-air balloons gave Strelzyk an idea. It might be possible to escape across the Iron Curtain at night in a balloon.

The friends built two balloons, but both failed.

Then they built a third balloon. Fearing that East German police would be looking for people buying large quantities of cloth, they acted in secrecy, traveling to different stores in neighboring towns to buy small amounts of nylon cloth.

It took more than two weeks to stitch all the pieces together. Finally, a huge balloon was completed. Numerous secret tests were made. The balloon proved strong enough to lift the four adults and four children off the ground.

Shortly before midnight on September 15, 1979, Peter Strelzyk and Gunther Wetzel drove into the countryside south of Possneck. Encouraged by a light breeze moving toward the Iron Curtain, the two men raced back to town. They collected their families and their balloon.

It was nearly 1 A.M. when they reached a spot about 9 or 10 miles (15 kilometers) from the Iron Curtain. Working quickly and quietly, they unpacked the balloon and crowded onto the little platform.

It was a chilly evening, and as the balloon rose the temperature dropped. Before long, the balloon had reached a height of 8,600 feet (2,600 meters) above sea level, and the temperature was about 18 degrees Fahrenheit (minus 8 degrees Celsius).

Suddenly a bright spotlight appeared from the ground. For an instant, the balloon was bathed in brilliant light. A moment later, darkness returned.

The passengers wondered if they had been spotted by East German border guards. They waited nervously for machine-gun fire, but none came. The great balloon continued drifting west.

Then about twenty-three minutes after liftoff, the gas burner began to sputter and die. The balloon fell slowly at first, and then faster. It landed with a thud in a berry patch.

Now, there was even more reason for fear. Where were they? Had they crossed over the Iron Curtain? Or were they still in East Germany?

The answer came almost immediately. A car came speeding toward them. It was an Audi, driven by West German police. The Iron Curtain had been crossed in a homemade balloon!

The Wetzel family and the Strelzyk family (inset) made a colorful balloon. After their daring escape, the East German government limited the amount of nylon and other lightweight fabrics that could be purchased by individuals.

The Wetzels and the Strelzyks became instant celebrities in West Germany and much of the world. But not a word about them was heard on East German newscasts. Only East Germans who tuned into West German radio and television stations learned about their daring escape.

In the years before and after the "great balloon escape," thousands of East Germans risked their lives to cross the Iron Curtain and escape to the

West. Some dug tunnels under the wall while others flew homemade airplanes over it. Many merely ran for their lives. No one knows how many people succeeded or how many were captured or killed trying.

Many people who stayed behind the Iron Curtain in Eastern Europe were equally dissatisfied with Communist rule. Over the years, their dissatisfaction grew. During the second half of 1989, political unrest and mass demonstrations increased dramatically in Poland, Hungary, Romania, Czechoslovakia, and East Germany. In all of these countries, and soon in Bulgaria and Yugoslavia as well, hard-line Communist governments were overthrown or forced to change.

East Germans march in Leipzig in 1989 demanding reforms and free elections.

Romanian demonstrators burn the Communist flag as they demand greater freedom. The sign at the right reads "Liberty" and "Revolution Continues."

Some of the changes in Eastern Europe were made possible by the Russian government led by Mikhail Gorbachev. For more than forty years, the Soviet Union had ruled the nations of Eastern Europe, including East Germany, with an iron fist. Now, beset by widespread poverty in Russia, Gorbachev called for sweeping changes. He tried to loosen his own nation's hold on its smaller neighbors. Those governments, in turn, stopped using deadly force along much of the Iron Curtain.

As soon as they were given the chance, people began cutting holes in the fortified boundaries. The first breaks appeared in the wall between Hungary and Austria, and soon Czechoslovakians were tearing down the walls wherever they could. Over the next few months, the once deadly Iron Curtain was virtually destroyed.

During the summer and early fall of 1989, the steady flow of people fleeing East Germany turned into a flood. First hundreds, and then thousands of Germans entered West Germany by crossing the Iron Curtain from Hungary, where the government allowed safe passage. In mid-September, sixteen thousand East Germans crossed through Czechoslovakia on their way to Hungary and freedom. From May through September 1989, about 50,000 people left East Germany. They had left

East Germans (left) sought refuge at the West German embassy in Prague, Czechoslovakia. An East German mother at the Prague embassy says good-bye to her daughter who went on to the West.

behind their homes, many of their loved ones, and nearly everything they owned. According to these new arrivals, many more East Germans, perhaps a majority of the nation's 16.6 million people, also desired to leave.

October 7, 1989, was East Germany's fortieth anniversary as a nation. But when what should have been the happy day arrived, Communist officials were in a state of shock. The mass exodus of their citizens was a tremendous embarrassment for them. Equally humiliating was the crumbling East German economy.

Erich Honecker

A few days after the nation's fortieth anniversary, East German Communist Party chairman Erich Honecker was forced to resign. On October 25, 1989, new GDR leader Egon Krenz announced that in the future it would be easier for East Germans to travel to the West. He also said that it would no longer be necessary for traveling East Germans to leave close family members behind as a guarantee that they would return to East Germany. But the promised reforms were not enough.

In early November, hundreds of thousands of East Germans gathered on the streets of East Berlin and other cities to demand changes in the nation's government. The Communist leaders knew that something had to be done quickly.

In 1989, the wall came tumbling down, and East Berliners were free to enter West Berlin.

On November 9, 1989, the East German government began to tear down the Berlin Wall. Jubilant East Germans, reporters, and television crews gathered at the once deadly site to celebrate.

There was great irony in the event. The wall had been built in 1961 to keep people in East Berlin from traveling to the West. Now it was being destroyed for that very same reason. Communist leaders hoped that, by allowing greater freedom, they could prevent East Germans from wanting to move to the West. For a time, the plan seemed to work. In the days that followed, millions of East Germans visited West Berlin, most for the first time. The majority returned home, hoping that conditions in East Germany would continue to improve.

The wall was made of thin but strong sections of reinforced concrete.

While the Berlin Wall was crumbling, the East German government began massive reforms. It promised free elections and a switch to a market economy—the type of free enterprise system that had made Western nations far more successful than Communist ones.

For decades, the powerless East German parliament had been under the political and economic control of the Communist Party leaders. But in mid-November, it suddenly came to life. The parliament elected Hans Modrow prime minister. Modrow called for more sweeping reforms and began hinting that East Germany might join West Germany to become a new nation.

Hundreds of East Germans pass through an opening in the Berlin Wall.

To the horror of Communist officials, it was becoming clear that many East Germans were continuing to move to the West. In November alone, 133,429 East Germans moved permanently to West Germany, and the total for the year, still incomplete, was nearly 330,000.

By early December, East Germany's Communist Party had lost much of its power. The Communist leaders even asked the United States government — no friend of Communists — to help keep it separate from West Germany.

As Communists continued to lose control of the nation, shocking discoveries were made. The East German secret police had kept files on millions of

A demonstrator shows an East German flag with the national emblem crossed out (left). East Germans stormed the secret-police headquarters and wrecked the offices.

East German citizens suspected of having anti-Communist opinions. In mid-January, 1990, an angry mob invaded the 3,000-room police headquarters, burning files and destroying furniture. Files that were not destroyed showed shocking abuses by the secret police.

It was learned that Communist authorities sold political prisoners to West Germany for as much as $60,000 per person. Some of this money was kept by government officials. Even more surprising, documents proved that Communist agents had long-standing contacts with most of the world's major terrorist organizations.

East Germans also learned that their Communist

rulers had lived like kings while ordinary people suffered. The vacation home of one leader was like a palace—at a time when most East Germans were forced to wait years for a tiny apartment.

Some former Communist leaders were suddenly in danger from their own people. Long-time party boss Erich Honecker was arrested, released briefly, and finally forced into hiding. By the end of January, East Germany's Communist Party was forced to share power with other political groups. To keep the government from collapsing, the nation's first democratic elections were scheduled for May 18, 1990.

Although the elections were still months away, nearly everyone realized that the Communist Party in East Germany was doomed. Prime Minister Hans Modrow began calling for unification with West Germany. In a speech given on February 7, 1991, West German chancellor Helmut Kohl suggested that West German money should start to be used in East Germany. The West German mark was one of the world's strongest currencies, while the East German mark was nearly worthless outside Communist nations.

Many people in both East and West Germany hoped that the two nations could be reunited soon. Leaders of the United States and the Soviet Union seemed to agree. On February 11, Mikhail Gorbachev met with Helmut Kohl. The Russian leader agreed that the question of unification should be decided by the German people. A day later, U.S. president George Bush publicly applauded Gorbachev's decision. The president also said that a united Germany would have to be a part of the North Atlantic Treaty Organization (NATO).

Since 1949, a number of North American and Western European nations had worked together to defend themselves against any attack by Communist nations. The political and military organization established for that defense was called NATO. West Germany joined the organization in 1955.

That same year, 1955, the Soviet Union, East Germany, and other Communist countries formed the Warsaw Treaty Organization, better known as

A conference at NATO headquarters in Brussels, Belgium

the Warsaw Pact. The Warsaw Pact was the Communist version of NATO. For thirty-five years, the two military alliances opposed each other. This period was called the Cold War.

Gorbachev felt that a united Germany should belong to both NATO and the Warsaw Pact, but Bush felt it could only be a part of NATO. The disagreement threatened to stop the reunification.

Another problem arose as well. For years, the Communist governments of East Germany and Poland had been arguing about their common border. Before World War II, territory east of the Oder and Neisse rivers was part of Germany. After Germany's defeat in 1945, this land became part of Poland and the two rivers formed the political boundary between Poland and Germany. However, many Germans felt that the Polish land rightfully belonged to Germany. For a time, therefore, Polish officials strongly objected to German unification, fearing that a stronger Germany would take control of the disputed land.

While these questions simmered, events moved quickly in the direction of German unity. A great deal of effort was spent trying to decide how best to join the economies of the two nations.

The factories of East Germany, the best in Europe before World War II, had declined dramatically. For

Environmental pollution is a serious problem in East Germany. This power plant uses high-sulfur coal, which greatly adds to air pollution.

example, in 1990, West German factories turned out some of the world's finest cars, including Audi and Mercedes-Benz. But East Germany produced only the poorly made, low-powered Trabant. Under communism, East Germans had learned that hard work seldom led to promotions and higher wages. The correct politics were far more important. Besides, the wages they were paid went mostly to buy goods produced in East Germany and other Communist countries. These goods were usually of poor quality and in such short supply they were difficult to purchase anyway.

How would the currencies of East and West Germany ever be converted to a single standard?

The answer came quickly. On March 14, 1990, West Germany's Helmut Kohl announced plans that would allow East Germans to exchange many of their nearly worthless East German marks for valuable West German marks on a one-to-one basis. The exchange would cost the West German government the equivalent of tens of billions of dollars.

On May 17, the West German government announced plans to spend $70 billion rebuilding East Germany's economy. The following day, May 18, representatives from the two Germanys signed a treaty spelling out all the details of the economic unification. It would take effect on July 1.

East Germans line up to exchange their currency for West German marks.

East Germans enter a polling place (left) for the first democratic election in over 40 years. Helmut Kohl (above) and Lothar de Maiziere (at left) toast Germany's economic unification.

On May 18, 1990, East Germans voted in their first free election since 1933. It was the first (and last) Western-style vote in the history of East Germany, and the results all but destroyed the power of the Communist Party. The biggest winners were a group of political parties backed by West German chancellor Helmut Kohl.

The new government of East Germany was determined. Its new prime minister, Lothar de Maiziere, called for unification. In the forty-year history of the German Democratic Republic, he was its only democratically elected leader.

By June, the hammer-and-compass coat of arms

of East Germany's Communist Party was removed from government buildings. The shoddy goods made in Communist factories began selling at fire-sale prices—few business people wanted to hang on to goods that would be almost worthless after the July 1 economic union. For the first time in over fifty years, West German and international corporations, including IBM, were planning to build offices, stores, and factories in East Germany.

On Sunday, July 1, 1990, the economies of East and West Germany were formally joined. Early the next morning, millions of East Germans converted their money to West German marks. That same day, July 2, the subway system between East and West Berlin was relinked for the first time since 1961.

Only two major problems remained, and both were solved within the month. The governments of East and West Germany had guaranteed that the existing border with Poland would be respected. On July 5, the Polish government gave up its insistence on a written treaty.

Soviet premier Gorbachev and West German chancellor Kohl met in Russia to discuss a unified Germany's role in NATO. During the two-day meeting, Gorbachev finally agreed to allow Germany to become a member of NATO only.

What seemed like an act of kindness by the Russian leader was actually shrewd politics. It was soon revealed that Gorbachev ended his objections only after Kohl promised Russia approximately $3 billion in much-needed foreign aid. Now virtually all the major obstacles to German unification were gone.

On September 13, foreign ministers from the United States, the Soviet Union, Great Britain, France, and East and West Germany met in Moscow. There, they signed a treaty in which the Allied nations of World War II formally surrendered their rights to occupy Germany.

On September 21, the parliaments of both East and West Germany overwhelmingly ratified a final treaty calling for German unification on October 3, 1990. Germans on both sides of what was once called the Iron Curtain looked toward the future with

Below: Mikhail Gorbachev (right) with Helmut Kohl. Right: Lothar de Maiziere (center) celebrates.

much excitement. The plans were soon finalized. The reunified country would officially be called the Federal Republic of Germany, the name of the old West Germany. The West German flag, national anthem, and constitution would now serve all Germans. Although it would take years to move government offices, the once-divided city of Berlin would again be the capital of the new Germany. Helmut Kohl was to become the reunited nation's first chancellor (head of state), and Richard von Weizsäcker its first president.

On the evening of Tuesday, October 2, 1990, a million people gathered in the streets of Berlin near the Reichstag, a building constructed in the late 1800s to house Germany's parliament. The people toasted the new nation and sang German songs. At the stroke of midnight, a copy of America's Liberty Bell rang in the new era of German life.

In a nearby concert hall, East German prime minister Lothar de Maiziere addressed the political and social leaders gathered there. It was his final act as an East German. "In a few moments," he said, "the German Democratic Republic accedes to the Federal Republic of Germany. With that, we Germans achieve unity in freedom. It is an hour of great joy. It is the end of many illusions. It is a farewell without tears."

A monument to
the four powers
that controlled
Berlin after
World War II.

INDEX

About the Author

Jim Hargrove has worked as a writer and editor for more than ten years. After serving as an editorial director for three Chicago area publishers, he began a career as an independent writer, preparing a series of books for children. He has contributed to works by nearly twenty different publishers. His Childrens Press titles include biographies of Mark Twain and Richard Nixon. With his wife and daughter, he lives in a small Illinois town near the Wisconsin border.